THE WORLD FOLKTALE LIBRARY

Tales from the British Isles

Tales from the British Isles

By John Greenway

Illustrated by Jan Palmer

Consultants

Moritz A. Jagendorf
Author and Folklorist

Carolyn W. Field
Coordinator of Work with Children
The Free Library of Philadelphia

SILVER BURDETT COMPANY

Morristown, New Jersey
Glenview, Ill. • Palo Alto • Dallas • Atlanta

INTRODUCTION

Folktales are not the creations of any particular author. They belong to the generations of people who pass the stories along from parent to child, from friend to friend, and from townsfolk to travelers. As they are told through the centuries, folktales change and grow. That is how they become rich with the sounds, smells, sights, and feelings that you will share.

These folktales were gathered from many places in the British Isles. The story called "Death in a Green Bag" came from a book by Geoffrey Chaucer. He was the first to write down this folktale nearly six hundred years ago when it was already very old. For two thousand years before Chaucer's time, this tale had been passed along by word of mouth.

Folktales are not usually about real people or actual events, but in a way they are true stories. They tell something important about the people and places from which the stories come. Even if you do not believe the ideas expressed in "Death in a Green Bag," you should remember that they are some people's true feelings about mischief play, evil characters, and death. For example, Irish people see variations of the way Gormless Tom behaves in many of their friends and neighbors. You may also know someone that reminds you of Gormless Tom. Perhaps you think that there is a little bit of Tom in all of us. In this way, a folktale is also a true story for you.

These folktales will make you laugh, cry, and smell the heather. Enjoy and share them. They will belong as much to you as to the people from whom they came.   THE EDITOR

Library of Congress Catalog Card Number: 78-56058   ISBN 0-382-03353-1

Table of Contents

Gormless Tom

In all of Ireland there was never a poor woman so unfortunate as the mother of Gormless Tom.

"Lawk-a-mercy!" she would say. "How very unlucky I am to have the greatest boob in all of Ireland for a son! He never has a thought in his head."

And it was true. Imagine a boy three times as old as you are, and three times as big. And he couldn't be sent alone to the fair on market day because of the thoughtless things he might do.

"Tom," said his mother one day, giving him a penny. "Go to the fair and buy a dish as big as a wagon wheel. On Sunday, we'll serve a fine dinner for our friends."

Tom skipped off with the penny. Soon he had bought a dish as big as the wheels on Jem Doyle's wagon.

" 'Tis a thought I have in me head," he said to himself. "The dish is so big that I'll save me strength and roll it home."

He had not rolled the dish far before it hit against a stone in the road and broke.

"Ah, well," thought Tom, "ten little dishes are as good as one big dish," and he carried the pieces home. " 'Tis a thought I have in me head that me mother will be pleased."

But his mother was as cross as a bagful of cats. "You great, gormless boob!" she cried. "Why didn't you have a thought to put the dish in the load of hay that Jem Doyle was after carrying home in his wagon?"

"Well, Mother," replied Tom sadly, "I'll have that thought in me head next time."

On the next market day Tom's mother gave him another penny. "Buy me a good pair of sewing needles," she told him, "and mind that you get them home safe and sound this time."

As he left the fair with the needles, Tom saw his neighbor, Jem Doyle, sitting on his cart with a great load of hay behind him. "Just the thing!" he thought, and he stuck the needles into the hay.

"Where are the needles?" asked his mother when Tom came home.

"Ah, Mother of mine," smiled Tom, "it's pleased you'll be with your son. I had a thought in me head to put the needles into Jem Doyle's hay as you said, and it's there you'll find them safe and sound."

"Tom, you great boob! Why didn't you stick the needles into your hat? Sure and we'll never find needles in a haystack."

"Ah well, Mother, I'll not complain. But it's you that told me to put the dish in a stack of hay. I'll have a thought in me head next time."

Tom kept his thought in his head when his mother sent him for butter on the next market day. He put the butter into his hat and put his hat on his head. This time he was lucky. He didn't lose the butter and he didn't break it. But it was a very hot day and the butter melted. It melted into his hair and down his face and onto his clothes.

Tom's mother shook like a wet dog in a sack, with the great anger in her. "Musha! You great noodle!" she scolded. "It would be better to have a thought in your head than butter dribbling down over it."

It was a long time before Tom was sent to the market again. But one day when there was no money in the house, his mother put a lamb into a basket. "Now, Tom," she ordered him, "take this wee lamb to market and get the highest penny for it." That was the Irish way of saying "get the highest price."

"Ah, Mother, never fear," said Tom. "'Tis a thought I have in me head that I'll get the highest penny."

"Make sure you do," warned his mother, "or you'll be sorry till your dying day, if you live that long."

At the market Tom stood with his basket at his feet, calling out, "Fine lamb for sale!" By and by a man came along and asked him what he wanted for the beast.

"Sure and me mother said she'll have me skin if I don't bring home the highest penny in the market," answered Tom.

"I'll give you a shilling for the lamb," said the man, "and that's a good price." And it was, for a shilling was worth twelve pennies.

"Are you sure it is the highest penny in the market?" asked Tom.

"Well," said the man, " 'tis a very high penny!"

A sly young lad who stood by listening to the bargaining pulled Tom by the sleeve. "No," he said, "that's not the highest penny in the market. I'll show you the highest penny in the market." And with that he took a penny from his pocket and climbed up a ladder. He held the penny high above Tom's head.

"Sure and it is the highest penny," said Tom doubtfully. "Even an eejit could see that plain enough." So Tom, poor boob, handed the sheep over

to the cunning boy and took the penny. "Ah," said Tom, " 'tis delighted me mother will be, for I have got the highest penny in the market."

When Tom gave his mother the penny, he got the highest lump on his head that ever he had. "Tom's mother is as foolish as Tom," said the neighbors, "to send him to market to be cheated." And so for a long time she kept him home.

But winter came, and the larder was empty. So Tom's mother decided to go to market herself. The old woman went to the fireplace where she had hidden her money. She took up a stone from the chimney and pulled a leather bag from its hiding hole. The bag was empty. All the money had been spent. "Musha, musha, musha," she sobbed. "It's no money we have, and Christmas is upon us! I'll have to sell our cow. 'Tis hardly a sadder thought I can imagine."

She put her thin shawl over her strong shoulders and went to the pasture. She took the cow by the halter, but the cow was stronger than she was. "I cannot pull this cow to market," she sighed. "I'll have to send Tom. More's the pity, for he hasn't a thought in his head. It's humbugged he'll be."

She called Tom to her. "Tom, Tom, me poor, gormless boy. I'll forgive you the dish and the needles and the butter and the lamb, if only you'll sell the cow for a pound. But a pound it must be, no less."

"Never fear again, Mother," smiled Tom. "It's a foolish, gormless boy I used to be, but now I have a thought in me head. I'll get a pound for the cow." So he took the cow by the halter and pulled her along, for he was strong in the arms even if he was weak in the head.

He had not gone three miles down the road when he saw a little old man in a great leather hat, sitting on a stone wall with a leather bag by his side.

"Is it Tom you'd be?" grinned the little old man. "Is it Clever Tom, the lad with the thought in his head?"

"Aye, it's me that I am, and that's no mistake," Tom answered. "And would you like to buy this cow for a pound?"

"Is it only a pound you want for that fine cow?" exclaimed the little old man, putting a frown on his old face. "Sure and it's worth more than that, it is. I'll give you this leather bag full of lovely old pennies, so I will, to please your old mother and yourself."

"Ah, 'tis humbuggin' me you'd be," said Tom
cautiously. "Them is only pennies, and it's a thought
in me head that it takes many pennies to make a
pound."

"Sure and it's a clever boy you are indeed," the
little old man laughed. "But these are not ordinary
pennies. Look at them!" He took a handful of coins
out of the bag and let them fall from his fingers.
They were the oldest pennies Tom had ever seen.
Black with age they were, and as they fell into the
bag they didn't sound like pennies.

"Sure and they're lovely old black pennies," agreed Tom, "but it's a pound I must have."

"Tom, Tom, you foolish boy," the little man said. "It's the old sayings that are never wrong, and you know that

> *An old dirty penny*
> *Is worth more than many.*"

"True it is," Tom answered, "but it's a pound that me mother means to have."

"And it's the worth of a pound you will have," nodded the old man, "for it's a true old saying that

> *A penny that's round*
> *Is worth more than a pound.*"

"Sure and it's round they are," Tom admitted, "but I still have a thought in me head that it's humbuggin' me ye are."

"Humbuggin' you, is it I am?" shouted the old man, hopping up and down in rage. "Sure and it's only one cow you'd be selling me, and it's a bagful of lovely old pennies I'd be giving you. You know the old saying

> *A penny and a half*
> *Buys a cow and a calf.*"

Poor Tom had never a thought in his head that the little old man was making up the sayings on the spot. He did not want to seem more ignorant than he was, so he said at last, "It's a true enough saying." He handed over the cow and took the bag of pennies.

Oh, what a wailing and weeping there was in the house when Tom brought home the bag of pennies! "It's the ruin of me," cried his poor old mother, "but I'll make it the dear ruinin' of you!" And she took the bag of pennies and flung it at his head. Tom wasn't so brainless but what he could duck — and so he did and the bag fell into the great pot of soup hanging over the fire.

"We've lost the cow and now we'll lose the soup," his mother wailed, and she snatched the bag from the pot and threw it on the floor. The old leather split open and the coins rolled out all over the rough boards. The soup had washed the black from them and there they lay, bright and shining.

"Lawk-a-mercy on me!" the old lady chortled. "It's not pennies they are, but gold pieces! We'll be the richest poor people in Ireland!"

And gold pieces they were indeed, worth more than all the pennies in the village and all the cows too, and all the dishes and all the lambs. Never was there a poor woman in all of Ireland so lucky that day as the mother of Gormless Tom.

And as for Tom, he never had to go to the market again, and he was happy the rest of his life with never a thought in his head.

You Can't Please Everybody

Do you know what happens when you try to please everybody? If you don't, just listen to the story of Angus MacNab, Sandy MacNab, and the donkey.

Angus MacNab was a Scotsman just a wee bit older than your father. Sandy was his son, just a wee bit younger than yourself. They were a pleasant and pleasing pair, and if they had a fault, it was trying to please everybody.

They lived in a cottage that was neither here nor there, by the side of a country road in the lowlands of Scotland. All along the sides of the road grew thistle, which the Scots love more than any other flower. If you are not a Scotsman, and if you have seen thistle, you will want to know why anybody would love such a prickly, stickly, ugly, struggly weed. But I cannot tell you, for I am not a Scotsman, and Scotsmen have never told anyone else in the world why they love the thistle.

Angus and Sandy MacNab had a donkey, and it loved thistle, too. It loved thistle so much that every day it went walking along the road eating all it could, prickles and stickles and all.

Scotsmen who traveled the road in front of the MacNabs' cottage saw the donkey eating thistle. It did not please them to see such a thing, and soon one of them knocked at the door of Angus MacNab.

"Auld mon!" he shouted when Angus opened the door. "Yon donkey's i' the thistle, and it's a disgrace to the nation—a donkey munching on the glory of Scotland."

"By my faith!" said Angus. "I wouldna want to displease the nation or yourself. I'll hae the beast oot o' there at once."

So Angus chased the donkey out of the thistle, for he would not displease a body for anything in the world. And to make sure the donkey would not go into the thistle again, he made a sign and put it on a pole just beyond the cottage. It read: DONKEY, DINNA EAT YON THISTLE.

But the donkey had been born in England and it couldn't read a word of a Scottish sign, so it just went on merrily eating the thistle.

And the passersby knocked on Angus' door and

complained again. "Why, 'tis monstrous, mon, a donkey dining on thistle!"

The only thing Angus could think of to keep the donkey out of the thistle was to build a big fence around his cottage and his little pasture. This kept the donkey out of the thistle well enough, but the first thing Angus knew, one of his neighbors was knocking on his door again.

"Hech, auld mon! Ye canna build a fence like that in Scotland. D'ye want to keep friends oot? That wouldna be a neighborly thing to do. 'Tis a disgrace to the nation."

So Angus, unwilling to displease his neighbors, took the fence down. That let the donkey into the thistle again, and again came the knocking and again the complaining.

Angus called his son to him. "Laddie, we canna keep the donkey oot o' the thistle, so to please everybody, we maun sell the donkey. Would it displease ye if we took the creature to market and sold it?"

"Nay, Father," answered Sandy, "let us sell the beast and please the neighbors."

They put a halter around the donkey's neck and started walking down the road, looking for a market

where they could sell the donkey. They had gone
only two hills from home when they met a farmer
coming from the opposite direction. He was riding
on a donkey.

"Are ye daft now, mon?" laughed the farmer.
"Walking when ye have a donkey! Canna ye ride?"

Angus was happy enough to walk, but as always
he wanted to please everybody, so he got up on the
donkey's back. The donkey was so short and Angus
was so tall that his shoes dragged along the ground.
The donkey was bothered never a bit, because
donkeys are sturdy and strong little animals, and
this one could carry five Angus MacNabs on its back,
if you could find so many.

Again a little while of walking and they came to
an old woman hobbling along the road ahead of

them. When she saw Angus riding the donkey she screeched. Angus looked at her. She was an old crone, and her head was covered by a shawl. All Angus could see was her long, sharp nose, which, as you will hear, she liked to stick into other people's business. And she gave a sniff with each stick.

"*Sniff*. Och, ye thochtless auld mon!" she sniffed. "Ye great lump, to sit on a donkey and let your poor son walk behind like a servant lad. *Sniff*. Get off, ye lump, and let the poor laddie ride. *Sniff*."

Angus wished to please the old woman, so without a word he got off the donkey, and without a word, Sandy got on. Clipper-clopper went the donkey down the road, with Sandy on its back and Angus after them.

Soon they passed another old woman. Her nose was longer and she sniffed twice as often. "Ou! What a disgrace to the nation! *Sniff, sniff*. A braw lump of a lad riding when his poor auld father must walk on his poor auld legs! *Sniff, sniff*. Let your poor auld father ride on the donkey, ye lump. *Sniff, sniff*."

Sandy was like his father and wished to please everybody, so he stopped the donkey and bade his father get up behind him. The donkey was just as glad to please everybody, for it scarcely noticed the weight of two riders. It just bobbed its head up and down a few times and thought of thistles as it clopper-clippered along the road.

A little farther and two women ran out of their cottage, scolding the travelers. "Shame on ye lumps o' loons, to sit baith o' ye on a poor auld donkey! It's the twa o' ye great lumps wha should be carrying the poor beast of an animal instead, it is!"

Angus and Sandy jumped off at once. Still wanting to please everybody, they lifted the donkey up on their shoulders. They made a strange sight — the father with the front of the donkey hanging over his shoulders, and the son with the animal's hind legs dangling down his back.

"By my faith!" complained Angus. "It's hard to please the world."

But they went along, just like that, the two stumbling under the weight of the donkey and growing more annoyed with pleasing the world at every step. The donkey was annoyed, too, with having to be carried, and it gave the MacNabs smart kicks with its sharp little hoofs.

They came to a bridge over a fast-rushing river and there, sitting on the edge of the bridge, was a crowd of young boys fishing. When the boys saw the queer procession, they dropped their fishing poles and laughed so hard that they had to lie down and roll around on the wooden bridge.

"Will ye look at the daft loons!" the boys said to one another. "Two donkeys carrying a third, and the smartest one on top! Did ye ever see the like in all the world?"

Too many straws will break a camel's back, as the old saying goes. And a rolling pack of laughing boys is enough to break the patience of even so gentle a man as Angus MacNab.

"Och! We've done all we can to please the world, and there's no thanks for it! Let us be free o' the burden, lad!" And with one will and one heave, Angus and Sandy threw the donkey into the water. The donkey traveled down that galloping stream all the way back to England, where it lived quite happily with nary a thistle. The MacNabs, father and son, trudged home and shut their door on this world that is so hard to please.

And that is how they learned a great truth which you may learn through their experience. When you try to please everybody, you please nobody, least of all yourself. And often you lose your donkey in the bargain.

Jack and the Cornish Giants

Once upon a time, and a very good time it was, there lived a smart young couple in the land of Cornwall. The lad was named Jack the Tailor. There was no happier person in all the world, unless it was his wife, Jill.

Jack's tailor shop was in front of their house, and he sat by the window all day, sewing and looking out upon the world as it passed by. Jill did her work in the house behind. Every few minutes, she would put down her work and go into the shop. There they would talk about things that made them both very glad. Oh, those were good days except for one thing —the giants of Cornwall.

The country was overrun by giants! They were very ferocious. When the thump of a giant's heavy footstep was heard, people would run inside and shut their doors. But this did not do much good. Each giant was so big, he could reach down the chimney or destroy a house with one blow of his club.

The most unpleasant thing about these huge fellows was that they were cannibals. They ate people. But although they were ferocious and fierce, the giants were a foolish lot with few brains. It made the people who were eaten very angry to be gobbled up by giants who were so stupid.

The King of Cornwall hated the giants more than anybody else did. Perhaps it was because he was so tiny himself. Perhaps it was because the giants were eating up all his subjects. Whatever the reason, he was always looking for somebody to kill the giants.

One lazy summer day when Jack the Tailor was sitting in his window sewing, a huge, black, hairy spider came creeping in through the door. Jack promptly threw his shoe at it and knocked it quite senseless.

"Jill!" he called. "Come here and see this giant of a spider. I've killed a giant!"

Just at that moment a busybody of a fellow passed by the window and heard Jack say, "I've killed a giant!"

The busybody ran to the palace and said to the King, "Jack the Tailor has just killed a giant."

"Just the man I've been looking for," the King chortled. He sent for Jack. "I hereby change your name from Jack the Tailor to Jack the Giant-Killer," said the King. "You are now the official giant-killer for the whole kingdom."

"But Your Majesty," began Jack, "it was only a very——"

"Silence when you are speaking to me!" the King commanded. "I want nothing out of you but silence, and very little of that. Now go out and kill the giants, every last one of 'em. And when you have killed them all, make sure none of 'em come back. Now off with your head. I mean, off with you!"

So Jack hurried home to tell his wife the news. "Jill! The King has ordered me to kill all the giants. Get me my giant-killing tools."

Jill hurried to the pantry and got out a shovel, a pickax, and a lamb's horn. The pantry was a strange place to keep such things, but we won't worry about that now.

Unless you live where there are monsters of this sort, you do not know what a lamb's horn is used for. But if there are giants in your town, you know that blowing on a lamb's horn is the best way to call up the big fellows.

"Well now, Jill my girl," said Jack, "your husband is off to kill his first giant. Wish me luck!" Jill kissed him and patted his hand, and Jack shouldered his

tools and walked out into the road.

Not far from their house stood the Mount of Cornwall, and it was there that Cormoran the giant lived. He was only a middling-sized giant, eighteen feet high at the head and nine feet around at the waist. He had eaten a good many Cornishmen in his time and hoped to eat a good many more.

Jack took the pickax and shovel and dug a hole nineteen feet deep in the middle of the road. He put branches and leaves across to hide it, but anyone could tell there was a pit underneath, unless that

anyone was a giant. Giants were far too stupid to
see anything as plain as a hole in the road.

Jack then put the lamb's horn to his lips and blew
on it as hard as he could. Cormoran was drowsing at
his dinner table on the Mount of Cornwall when the
horn blew. He had just finished eating the tastiest,
fattest Cornishman he had eaten for many a day,
and he was sleepy. But when he heard the blast of
the horn, he got up and lumbered down the road.
Thump, thump, thump, thump went his heavy feet.
The Cornish people heard the noise and felt the

ground shake, and they all went into their houses and shut the windows. All except Jack, who stood boldly at the side of the road, waiting. Soon he heard Cormoran crashing down the road toward him. Thump! Thump! Thump! Thump!

The giant came closer and closer and faster and faster when he saw Jack. He was not really hungry after eating so fat a Cornishman, but he thought Jack would make a delicious little dessert. Thumpthumpthumpthumpthump, he ran. Then thumpthumpthumpthump CRASH! Down through the branches and leaves went the stupid giant, and there he was standing at the bottom of the hole.

Jack took out a pencil and paper. He wrote down "19," which was the depth of the hole. Then he wrote "18," which was the height of the giant. He wrote them down like this:

$$\begin{array}{r} 19 \\ -18 \\ \hline 1 \end{array}$$

"It's a good thing I learned my arithmetic. Since the giant's head is one foot below the top of the hole, I think I can safely give him a great whack with my pickax."

He gave the giant a whopping good crack and

broke his crown. Then Jack took the shovel and filled up the hole around the giant. It was a very neat job. "That's one of 'em," he said. "I'll leave the others for tomorrow."

The other giants were very angry when they heard the news. From all over Cornwall they came, and from Wales too, and they met in Cormoran's empty castle. There they ate all the Cornishmen in sight while they talked about Jack the Giant-Killer.

"There's no sense in us all goin' after this Jack," said the smartest giant. "Let's just send the biggest and fiercest of all us giants to kill him. Then the rest of us can eat Cornishmen in peace."

"Daah," said all the giants with great, foolish grins.

"We send Blunderbore. He's the biggest of all and he has two heads. Two heads are better than one."

One of Blunderbore's heads said it didn't like the idea very much, but the other one was hungry and won the argument. So Blunderbore thumped down the road to Jack's house.

Jack and Jill heard the giant coming. "Don't worry, dear husband," said Jill. "Just get into bed quickly." Then Jill covered him over so that only his face could be seen.

Thump! Thump! Thump! Thump! THUMP! The house shook, the dishes rattled, the spoons danced on the table. But just the same, Jill set about making pancakes, and into each one she put a round, iron stove lid.

The giant tapped on the door with his fingernail. BANG BANG BANG BANG! Jill ran to the door. "Good morning, Mr. Giant. Jack is not at home, and I am making pancakes for our baby's breakfast. Will you have some?"

"I wants Jack's plut," said the giant, meaning *blood*. "But I will eat some pancakes first, look you."

So Jill gave him two of the hard pancakes, one for each head. Blunderbore took two big bites and CRACK! All his teeth rattled out onto the ground.

"Hot's plut!" shouted Blunderbore. "Hard pancakes!"

"Middling hard, Mr. Giant. Our little baby is teething now and these pancakes help his teeth grow. See?" And she gave Jack a plain pancake without a stove lid in it.

Jack put on a big babyish grin. He said, "Goooo." And he gobbled up the pancake.

"Hot's plut! What a baby!" the giant Blunderbore said in amazement.

"Yes, he has the strongest white teeth from eating hard pancakes," said Jill. "Would you like to feel them?"

"I would, I would!" And the stupid big fellow put his finger in Jack's mouth.

Jack bit the finger as hard as ever he could.

"UH-GOO!" howled the giant.

"Well!" said Jill. "You cannot eat the pancakes I give to Jack's baby, and now Jack's baby has bitten your finger. I think it would be wise for you not to wait for Jack himself."

Blunderbore hurried out the door and thumped up the road to the castle on the Mount of Cornwall, where the other giants waited for him. They called Blunderbore a great booby and a coward, and they ordered him to try again to get rid of Jack the Giant-Killer.

"Daah," they said. "Invite him to the castle for supper and the night, and bash out his brains while he is sleeping."

Blunderbore's heads were aching too much for him to argue. So the giants all got together and set their big empty heads to work writing an invitation. They took a tree trunk and sharpened the end. They stuck the point in the ashes to make it black like charcoal, and they wrote a note on a big sheepskin.

Then late at night one of them thumped as quietly as he could to Jack's door and left the message. Then he thumped back to the castle as quietly as an elephant.

When Jack read the invitation, he decided to go. But first he made a big leather bag. He sewed it this way and he sewed it that way, until it fit under his coat as snug as you please. The mouth of the bag stuck out just above his shirt collar. As the sun slid over the west of the world, Jack took the sharpest knife from Jill's kitchen and started up the road to the Mount of Cornwall.

Meanwhile the giants had made themselves a great mess of lobscouse and tralliwaggers to celebrate what they were sure would be Jack's funeral. They were laughing and shouting with giantly glee when suddenly they heard Jack's knock on the kitchen door. Quickly they all hid, and made Blunderbore go to the door.

"Come in for good supper, Jack," muttered Blunderbore.

Jack came in as sprightly as you please and sat down at the table, which was so big that all you could see over the top of it were Jack's eyes. The giant was not able to see the mouth of the bag sticking out of Jack's collar.

"Have some lobscouse and tralliwaggers," said Blunderbore slyly, thinking giants' food would not agree with Jack.

"Poor food in a poor house," said Jack. "Still, I'm so hungry I could eat a giant."

This frightened Blunderbore so much that he stuffed both of his heads full of lobscouse and tralliwaggers. Two heads could eat more than one stomach could hold, and in no time at all the giant was filled to bulging. Meanwhile Jack was putting his food into the bag, so that he seemed to eat just as much as the giant.

"I will bust," Blunderbore said finally.

"No need for that," said Jack. "Do what I do. Make room for more."

He stood up so the giant could see him, and he stuck his knife into his shirt and cut open the bag so that all the lobscouse fell out, and a few tralliwaggers too. Then Jack gave the knife to Blunderbore.

"I can make room in my belly, too," said the giant. And he took the knife and plunged it into his belly and ripped it open from top to bottom and from side to side. Out dropped the lobscouse and tralliwaggers, and then out fell his very own tripes and trullibubs. By the time either of his stupid brains realized what had happened, he fell dead to the floor.

"That's another one," sighed Jack. "I think I'll leave the rest for another day." And he skipped off home, whistling merrily.

The other giants watched Jack leave. From their hiding places in the castle towers, they ran to the kitchen. There they saw Blunderbore lying dead, his tripes and trullibubs all over the floor. In great terror, the giants fled the castle. As they ran down the lane, all Cornwall shook for the very last time.

There was a great celebration throughout the land. The King invited Jack and Jill to live in his guest house. But they went back to their home in the village, instead. Once again they could pass the days talking about things that made them very glad.

The Clever Men of Gotham

Ever since the time of bad King John, seven hundred years ago, the people of Gotham have done just as they pleased. And the sillier a thing was, the more pleased they have been to do it. As you know, there is no happier head than one filled with feathers. It's brains that make all the trouble. Well, there was none of that trouble in Gotham!

The women happily wasted their days trying to gather up sunlight to make their homes bright at night. Many of them peered into mirrors with their eyes closed to see how they looked when they were asleep. And the men were no better, as you will see.

One fine summer day, twelve of the silly men of Gotham strolled along over to the little river that meandered slowly through their silly town.

"Let us go fishing," said one.

"A very happy thought," agreed another.

They pulled branches from the willow trees to make fishing poles, and they left the leaves on to make fishing lines. They had no hooks, but that was just as well, for they didn't want to hurt the fish.

Instead they tied oranges and apples to the branches and let them down into the water.

"Oranges and apples will be a fine treat for the fishes," said the silly men of Gotham. "We shall catch many dozen today." But of course you know they didn't.

They spent all that lazy afternoon wading in the stream and dragging their bobbing oranges and apples about in the water. "Ah, these fishes are stupid," said one of the silly Gothamites, as the day droned on with never a bite.

"Perhaps we should have peeled the oranges for them," said another.

"Aye, that's it," said a third. "We'll come back tomorrow and throw the peelings in, so they'll know we've prepared the fruit for them."

Very pleased with their cleverness, the twelve men of Gotham climbed out of the water. They put on their shoes and dropped their fishing poles and set off for home.

Suddenly the leader shouted, "Stop!"

"What's the matter?" asked the rest, piling to a halt behind him.

"One of us is missing!" said he. "There were twelve of us went out to the river and only eleven is a-coming back." They looked at each other with wild surprise, but they couldn't tell which one was missing.

"Let us count us," said the first man of Gotham. "Line up over there in front of me and I'll count us."

So the eleven of them lined up in front of him and he counted out loud. He counted slowly and he pointed his finger at each man in turn. "One. Two. Three. Four. Five. Six. Seven. . . ." And then, "Eight, nine, ten, eleven. You see?" he cried, too silly to point to himself and count twelve. "There's only eleven!"

"Only eleven?" they all cried. "Oh, one of us is drownded!" moaned the silly men of Gotham.

"Oh, poor which one of us," cried the leader. "Let us go back and drag the river for the unhappy drownded man."

Back they ran, wailing and weeping for the one of them that was missing. When they got to the river, some of them took off their shoes and some

didn't, but they all walked up and down in the water. It was only two feet deep, so they hardly got their knees wet. They poked about the reeds and called out for the drowned man to say where he was. They made an awful commotion with their weeping and wailing and splashing about.

After a time a man from another town came rowing down the stream and heard all the fuss. "Ho! Good men!" he shouted to them. "What's the trouble?"

"Alackaday! One of us is drownded," cried the men of Gotham, "and we don't know which one of us it is. It might be any of us!"

"It might be me!" wailed one of them.

"Or me!" wailed another.

"If you don't know which one of you it is, how do you know one of you is drowned?" asked the man.

"Because we counted us and there should be twelve of us and there is only eleven of us," they bawled.

The man in the boat was not from Gotham, so he saw quickly enough that there were indeed twelve of them. But he knew how silly the people of Gotham were. He decided he could have some fun, make a little money, and even save a drowned man. So he called, "Good men of Gotham, what will you give if I find the one of you that is missing, and save him?"

"Oh, sir, we'll give all the money in our pockets to get him back. We loved him better than any of us, although we don't know which one of us he was!"

The man rowed his boat to the shore and tied it up. Then one by one he helped the men of Gotham climb out onto the bank of the stream. "There now," he said, "I have saved the one of you that was drowned."

"But how do we know?" they cried.

"Line up," he replied. "I will touch each man with my oar and count as I go. Then you will know by the feel of the oar and the hearing of the count whether you are all here."

Then he took up his oar and whacked the first Gothamite so hard on the shoulder that the silly creature sprawled into the stream with a great splash. "That's one," the man shouted.

"Ah, yes, that's one," said the men of Gotham.

Then he gave the next a mighty swipe with the oar and knocked him rolling down the riverbank.

"That's two!" he called out.

And warming to his work, the boatman laid about him with his oar both hard and strong. Soon all

twelve of the Gotham men were floundering in the water and moaning with the hurt in their bones.

"Now," laughed the man, leaning on his oar, "I've counted all twelve of you and well you all know it. So the drowned man is safe again."

"Oh, the blessings of our heart go out to you, kind sir," said the Gothamites as they struggled out of the water. "Here is all the money we have. You have saved the very dearest one of us that was drownded, and we owe you all that we can pay."

And full of happiness and bruises but just as empty of brains as ever, they set off arm in arm for Gotham, where they remain as silly to this day.

How Greed Caught a Thief

This is the story of how greed caught a thief in the misty hills of Scotland many long years ago. The thief was known as "Greedy Gut," for not only did he steal and rob, but he gobbled all the food in a house as well. He never would leave a pie, a plate, a pin, or a plaid. His greed made him steal all he could carry and eat all he could hold.

He carried a long and heavy knobbly club, and a big basket that the Scottish people call a "creel." He used the club to pound on the door of a cottage and frighten the women when the goodman of the house was away. He used the creel to carry off all he could lift, which was a great deal, for he was a big man and strong. Even the bravest woman was terrified when she heard the club on her door and the roaring voice of the robber.

"Aaargh! I'm the notrocious Greedy Gut and I've a creel to fill, or a woman to kill if ye canna fill it!"

You might think that a robber with a heavy creel to carry would be easy to catch. But Greedy Gut was hard to catch because he was cunning, and always left himself plenty of time to escape before the goodmen could get home.

So it was one day that Greedy Gut crouched in a hiding place and watched by a wee cottage standing all alone near a peat bog. He saw the goodman and his son leave the cottage and trudge down the long road to the village, miles away. Then out he came, swinging his great club. He battered the door so hard the whole house shook and shivered.

"Aaargh! I'm the notrocious Greedy Gut and I've a creel to fill, or a woman to kill if ye canna fill it!"

Inside the house the woman and her three daughters, whose names were Kitty, Katty, and Katy, quivered in fear. But the mother was not so frightened that she lost all her wits, as you will see.

She quickly took her youngest daughter to the back window and whispered, "Katy, love, climb out as fast as you can and run to the village. Tell Da and your brother Kory to come and catch a thief."

"But Mither," cried Katy, "the village is so far awa' that the robber will be safe in the hills before Da and Kory can come back."

"Whisht, bairn, and you'll see. This robber is Greedy Gut, and his greed wilna let him go. He'll no' run far before the guidmen will catch him in the glen. Run awa', lassie, run awa'!"

So out the window jumped Katy and fast she ran down the road.

"Aaargh!" the robber shouted, still pounding on the door with his club. "Let me in before I break the door aboon ye!"

What else could they do but let him in? He growled at them and shook his club. Then he jumped about the room, filling his creel with all he could put his great hairy hands on. Spoons and forks of silver, plates of china, handkerchiefs of silk, candlesticks,

brooms, even the kettle off the hob—all went into his creel. And all the while he stole and packed, he gobbled—curds and cream and chunks of bread and cheese. He staggered with the weight of the creel as he went out the door, but never a spoon did he drop. And though his fists were still busy at his mouth, not one morsel did he spill.

"Ah, Mither," cried Kitty when the robber had gone. "Whatever shall we do? He's ta'en everything."

"One wee thing he missed, lassie, and I'm thinking that will catch him. See here!" And she went to the closet. There in a dark corner was her husband's finest pair of boots. "Let the great brute of a robber get awa' out of sight," said she, "and then we will run ahead by the side paths and get back the creel."

Katty and Kitty held their heads and cried. "Oh, Mither, he will murder us if we go near him!"

"Never fear, my bairnies. His greed will help us. Now be quick! And bring along a wee bag of salt."

So Katty and Kitty and their mother took the boots and the salt and ran along a shortcut through the heather. It was easy for them to get ahead of Greedy Gut, for they knew the way; and as for him, the weight of the heavy creel and his full stomach made him walk slowly.

Soon they were too far ahead for him to see them. Quickly the woman darted out and put one of the boots in the middle of the road. "Now, lassies, let us hurry along with the other boot and the salt."

By and by Greedy Gut came along and saw the boot in the road. "Aaargh!" he growled in robberly glee. "What a bonnie, sonsie boot!"

He put down his creel and his club and sat by the side of the road. He took off one of his shoes and pulled on the boot. It fit him as close as the whiskers on his own face, and that made him very angry.

"A curse on the rascal that left only one boot!" he snarled. "I might as well have one half a pair of scissors or half a pair of breeches!"

He pulled off the boot and threw it down on the road again. Then he put on his old shoe and gave the boot a savage kick. He took up his club and his creel and staggered on his way up the road.

Far ahead of him again by this time, the woman and her daughters were setting the second part of the trap for Greedy Gut.

"We'll leave the other boot here, children of mine. And we'll put a wee, bonnie sprinkle of salt in it for the sake of his foot." She put down the boot and quickly shook the salt into it. Then she turned and

smiled at Kitty and Katty.

"Now, Katty, run down the side path again and take away the first boot and hide it well. Kitty and I will have the robber's creel in less than no time!" As Katty sped away, Kitty and her mother hid in the gorse bushes.

Soon Greedy Gut came along. He saw the second boot in the road. "Aaargh! Now double curses on the villain who put the boots so far apart! I must have both boots! I couldna bear to lose such a prize!"

He sat down by the side of the road and took off his shoe. "Now that I have this boot, I might as well put it on, for I will have the second one in a minute. It'll be but a short walk to reach it, and I dinna care if I hobble a bit until then."

He stood up wearing the one boot. "Och, that's a mite close fit to my foot, but never mind. It's a bonnie pair of boots I'll have." He started to pick up his stick and creel. "Nay, they're a wee bit heavy. I'll just leave my club and creel and one shoe here in the road for the small time that I'll be gone." And off he trudged, a little gingerly, back the way he had come.

No sooner was he out of sight than Kitty and her mother popped out of the gorse and dragged the creel to a hiding place where the robber would never spy it. And they did not forget to take the cast-off shoe that Greedy Gut had left.

Can you imagine what Greedy Gut said when he got back to where the first boot had been? There was never a robber in all the world so angry. He roared and stamped and oh how that hurt his feet! All he wanted was to get back to his other shoe and his creel and his club. If you want to know how slowly he had to walk now, just you put on one shoe and one boot. But don't put any salt in the boot, for your foot would hurt more than would please you. You would limp and hobble and cry and say a naughty word or two, just like Greedy Gut, who raged and sobbed and stumbled along.

At last he came to the spot where he had left the shoe and the club and the well-filled creel. He stopped and he stared at the empty road. He stared. He blinked his eyes and shook his head and stared again. Then "Aaargh!" he bellowed, and "Aaargh!" again. He tore at the bushes and beat at the stones and

threw himself on the ground and kicked his legs.

He was still there roaring and growling and howling with rage when the goodman and his son came along and found him. They fell upon him with sticks and stones and beat him till he had a shirtful of sore bones to match his sore feet.

"You will never rob our women again," they promised him, "for we have caught you at last."

But they were wrong, you see. It was not really the men who caught Greedy Gut. It was his own greed that did—and a canny Scotswoman who knew how to turn it against him.

Jack and His Friends

In the bad days of Ireland when famine was on all the land, there lived a widow and her only son, whose name was Jack. A few potatoes were all they had left to eat, not near enough for the two of them. So one day Jack said to his mother, "Mother of mine, I'll go away and look for luck. If I find it, then sure and I'll be back to make you rich and happy."

He kissed his mother and took one potato to keep him alive till he met with luck. Down the road he started, with his potato in his pocket and his mother's tearful eyes upon him until he was out of her sight.

All the day he trudged along, but never a bit of luck did he find. The sun beat upon his back and the dust of the road covered his clothes, and it was sad he was so far from home.

As he passed a bog, he heard someone call in a loud, strange voice, "Hee-aw, could ye come and pull me-aw out of this bog before I be drowned and all? 'Tis all four feet of me that's stuck in it."

"Now what kind of a man would it be with four feet?" wondered Jack. "Sure and there are strange things in this country." But he was a kindly boy, and he walked over to the bog. There he saw a donkey, up to its knees in the spongy swamp and sinking before his eyes. Without a moment's delay, Jack began to throw branches and leaves in front of the beast.

"Step up on these, will you, whilst I pull you by the ears as hard as ever I can," ordered Jack.

Now a good pull by the ears will get anyone out of a swamp, and it was no time at all before the poor donkey was out on dry ground and thanking Jack for his service.

"It's mee-haw life you've saved," brayed the donkey, "and it's your servant I'll be-aw, if you want the havin' of me."

"Sure and it's nothing at all you owe me," replied Jack, "but it would be a fine thing to have your company whilst I look for luck."

"I could use a bit of luck meself," said the donkey, shaking his sore ears. "Let's go along together, you and meee-haww."

So off they went till they came to a village, where they heard the greatest rush of a row of noise. It was a poor old dog with a pot tied to his tail, flying down the road in a cloud of dust and noise and nasty boys.

"That's no way to treat a poor beast of a dog," said the donkey.

"Faith and it isn't," agreed Jack.

The donkey brayed and Jack shouted and they both ran at the boys. In a moment the young rascals and their dust were going the other way.

"Oh-oooo, thank you, gentlemen," howled the dog as Jack untied the pot from his tail. "They hit me with their sticks, so-hoooo they did, and it is a great shame, so it is."

"Come along with Jack and me-aw," invited the donkey, "for this is no town for the likes of you."

The three of them hadn't gone far beyond the village when the thinnest bag of bones of a poor old cat crept out onto the road in front of them.

"Do yez have the least bit of a bite of somethin' to eat-eeow for a poor ould cat starvin' to death for hunger of some food to eat-eeow?" the cat wailed.

"Would you care for a bit of potato?" asked Jack.

"Well, nee-ow, it's not me usual eatin', but a cat can't be critical. 'Tis somethin' to eat for all that."

You never saw a cat chew on a potato so hungrily! And you never heard a cat say "thank you-eeow" so heartily.

"Come alooong with us," the dog said, "and help

the lot of us look for luck."

"Well, nee-ow," meowed the cat, "if I can eat potatoes I can travel with dogs. And any-hee-ow, four heads are better than three when you're lookin' for luck."

At sundown they passed an old farmhouse, and there they saw some chickens settling down to roost for the night. Suddenly there was a commotion in the henhouse, and a red fox jumped out with something flapping in his jaws.

"Another villain!" barked the dog sharply. "The country is alive with scoundrels. Let go-hoo-ooo of that poor wretch of a roo-hoo-ster, or I'll have your tail for a duster!"

It would be a foolish fox with his mouth full of rooster to argue with a dog who spoke like that. The fox thought about the situation for a quarter of a second. Then he dropped the rooster and bounded out of sight across the field. The rooster fluttered to his feet, shook out his feathers, and shook hands with the dog.

"I never thought I'd be shaking hands with a dog-a-doodle-do," crowed the rooster, "but it's a real pleasure to do-de-doodle-do it, so it is."

"Then come along with us and help us look for

luck," said Jack and his friends all together.

"Sure and I will, neighbors, and proud I'll be to doodle-doodle-do it," said the rooster.

So the rooster and the cat and the dog and the donkey and Jack went off into the night. Nary a place did they see to have their sleep till they spied a glimmer of a glint of a light off in a field.

"Let's go and have the least bit of a look," the cat advised. "Sure and there might be-ow the kindest sort of a gentleman who would have a bed for a boy and a cat and a dog and a donkey and a rooster."

The five friends stepped off the road and stumbled in the dark across the field toward the light. The light was in a window. The window was in a house. And from the house came the laughter and shouting of a pack of ruffians.

"This does not sound like the house of the kindest sort of gentleman," said Jack. "We'd better have the least bit of a look before we knock on the door."

He crept up to the window and peered in, and so did the donkey. The dog jumped on the donkey's back, the cat jumped on the dog's back, and the rooster jumped on the cat's back, and they all looked in. What on earth do you think they saw? They saw a crowd of villainous rogues — a roostful of robbers — all sitting around a table heaped with gold and silver and food and drink.

"Begorra!" Jack whispered to his friends. "It's the rogues that robbed the Lord of Dunlavin a week ago last Tuesday. Sure and you heard about that villainous deed? They left the poor man penniless."

"Shameful!" said the dog.

"They're very rough creatures," agreed the cat.

"Let's frighten them out of their wits," said the donkey.

'Twas no sooner said than done. "Up with your blunderbusses, men!" shouted Jack. "Take the heads off 'em! Fire!"

The cat screeched and the dog howled and the rooster crowed and the donkey gave such a hee-haw as you never heard a donkey give before. And Jack smashed in the window and shouted, "Break their bones! Don't leave one of 'em alive to tell the tale!"

The robbers jumped up in the greatest fright and exploded out the back door, and ran across the fields as fast as ever you saw robbers run.

"Now we have a place to sleep and some food to eat," said Jack, "and first thing in the morning we'll take the gold and silver back to the Lord of Dunlavin."

"The proper thing to doodle-doodle-do," the rooster crowed.

It was a fine meal the hungry friends had, while all the time the robbers sat out in the damp, cold field, wondering what had happened.

"I'm cold," said one.

"I'm hungry," said another.

"I'm thinkin' we left too fast," said a third.

"There's nary a one of us shot, for all the noise," added a fourth.

"This is no way for robbers to live," said a fifth.

"Let's send Goby back and see what made all the fuss and commotion and rowdy-dow," said the captain of the thieves.

Goby's real name was Go-by-the-Wall-and-Tickle-the-Bricks. It's a name the Irish give to any sort of a kind of sneaky fellow who slinks by walls and won't walk in the open. Goby was just that kind of weeny rascal. He didn't much want to go back to the house, but the others helped him along with several good kicks. He crept up to the door as quiet as a little mouse, but the cat's sharp ears heard him.

"They're sneakin' back," the cat warned.

"Let's turn out the light and give them a welcome," Jack said.

Goby pushed open the door with never the sound of a squeak and crept in. Nary a sound!

And then suddenly the cat jumped on his head and dug her claws into his scalp. The dog sank his old teeth hard in Goby's leg. The rooster flew at him and pecked him with his beak and gashed him with his spurs. Jack belabored him with a stout broomstick. And as Goby ran out the door, the donkey gave him such a great kick that he had little walking to do to get back to the other robbers.

"And is it safe we'd be to go back?" the captain asked Goby.

"Safe is it you ask?" moaned Goby. "Sure and 'tis the devil himself with all his imps in that house. A demon of a fiend jumped on me head and tried to scratch out me eyes, and I don't believe he left more than two of them in me head. And another little imp with wings flew all around me, sticking me with eleven sharp knives. There's not a part of me without a hole in it! The devil himself beat me with a club as big as a fence post. And ten little devils crunched the poor bones of me poor legs with their great, slatherin' fangs! And at last the devil's own blacksmith gave me a blow with two of his sledgehammers that sent me flyin' through the air!"

"Sure and 'tis an awful-lookin' mess ye are!" said the captain, holding a candle up to the rascal's bleeding head. "I'm thinkin' it might be best for the lot of us to leave Ireland altogether. 'Tis little taste I have for conversin' with devils and imps."

But by the time he had said all that, there was no one left to hear him. The other robbers had already run away to Cornwall, where a good many of them remain to this day.

It was a long walk the morning after for Jack and his friends to the castle of the Lord of Dunlavin. The lord himself came out to see the strange collection of visitors.

"Sure and you're a queer lot for a body to see in the mornin'," said the Lord of Dunlavin.

"But a welcome lot for all that," replied Jack, "for here we have the gold and silver that the robbers stole from you Tuesday a week ago, leaving you the poorest rich lord in all of Ireland. 'Twas our thought you'd be glad to see it again."

"Glad is it?" chortled the Lord of Dunlavin. "Sure and 'tis so glad I am that I'll give you enough gold and silver so you'll never have to crow or howl or complain all the days of your lives."

And the lord was true to his word. The donkey got the finest stable and the rooster got the finest henhouse and the dog got the finest doghouse they had ever seen. And the cat grew fat on the thickest cream, while Jack's poor old mother never saw potatoes anymore for all the meat and peas and gravy that were over them. And they all lived to be a hundred and eight years old, with a bit of luck on every day of their lives.

Death in a Green Bag

This tale of three evil young men was told more than 500 years ago by Geoffrey Chaucer, one of England's own poets. It happened in the most terrible year in all the history of the world, when the Black Death crept into Europe. At that time three ships came to Italy with spices from China. In the hold of each ship were rats. And in the black fur of the rats the Black Death lay hiding.

The rats ran down the ropes of the ships to the docks and crept into the warehouses. At night they scurried into the houses of men and gave them the awful sickness. This Black Death took rich and poor alike, as if there were no difference between them.

Great fear came into men's hearts with the Black Death. Good men became better and bad men became worse. So it was with four bad young men who had spent their lives doing wicked things. If they met a man alone, they would fall on him with their daggers. When he lay dead, they would take his money and go to the taverns. There they would drink and gamble till the gold was gone.

At last came the day when the Black Death took one of these ruffians. His blood ran hot and lumps grew under his arms. Then his skin turned black and he died. The three villains who were left alive saw their friend being carried away to the grave.

"What has happened to our friend?" asked the first young man.

"Death has taken him away," said one of the men carrying the coffin, "and he is gone forever."

"Where is this Death?" asked the second villain.

"Yes, we will deal with him," the third young man blustered in his rage. "We will kill Death."

But no one could tell the three young villains where to find Death. They went from tavern to tavern, shouting and breaking cups. They seized men by the shoulders and shook them and shouted, "Where is Death?" No one hindered them for fear of their daggers. But no one could answer the question.

They left the last tavern on the edge of town and staggered along the crooked forest road. They cursed and called out for Death to show himself.

The day was dark and clouds hung low over the earth, rolling and rumbling as if the Black Death itself were in them. The only sound was the distant wailing of the townspeople whose loved ones had died.

As the three ruffians stumbled along, suddenly they saw a little old man sitting by the side of the road. His clothes were all as green as the grassy bank he sat on. He was not like the men in the taverns, for he showed no fear of the three young villains. He just sat and grinned at them.

"Old man!" roared the youngest of the three. "Where can we find Death?"

"Death is not found; he finds," laughed the little man in green.

"We want no riddles," the oldest ruffian cursed. "Tell us where we can find Death or we'll kill you."

"Death is not yet for me," the old man smiled. "I knock on the ground with my staff every evening and say, 'Dear Mother, let me in,' but still I go on living. It may be different for you young men, and so I will tell you where you can find Death."

The old man pointed down the road. "Go along this crooked lane," he said, "until you see a green apple tree with its branches hanging low. Near its trunk, you will find Death." He pulled his green hood over his forehead and gathered his green cloak around his chin, until all they could see of him was a grin on his leathery face, and his green eyes glittering.

The three ruffians ran along the road, their daggers in their hands. Soon they came to a tree, with its low branches heavy with apples as green as the clothes of the little old man. Under the tree they saw the green grass, and nothing else. The evil companions stopped and whispered to each other.

"The old man lied. Death is not here."

"Perhaps he is hiding behind the tree to take us by surprise."

With hatred in their hearts, they crept around the tree. When they met at the other side of the apple tree, they saw not Death but a bag made of green cloth. They opened the bag carefully. When they saw what was in it, they forgot all about their search for Death, for the bag was full of golden coins.

"I've never seen so much gold!" laughed the youngest. "We can buy all the wine in the town."

The other two were too full of glee to say anything. But such mirth does not last long, for the glee of gold is the joy of a moment. Soon the three villainous friends sat down and began to argue about what they might do with their wealth.

"Let us go back into the town and begin our

pleasure," said the man who was neither the oldest nor the youngest but the most foolish.

"No," replied the oldest, who was also the wisest and the most wicked. "We are not trusted in town. Men will say we stole it, and they will hang us."

"That is truth," the youngest villain scowled.

"Let us wait here until nightfall," the oldest went on. "Meanwhile, one of us must buy food and drink to keep us full and merry till the evening."

But none of the three trusted the others well enough to leave the treasure. Finally, the oldest villain suggested a choosing by lot.

"We will take three blades of grass, one shorter than the others, and each of us will draw blindly. The man who chooses the short blade must go to town."

The short blade of grass fell to the youngest of the villains and he left, complaining and grumbling against the others. When he was out of sight, the oldest rogue put his hand on the other's arm.

"Dear friend," he said, "you and I were always the closest of companions. This other fellow is not so dear to us. You heard his grumbling. There are 400 pieces of gold in this bag. If we divide them in two, you and I will have 200 gold coins each, enough to let us live merry for a year and more. If we divide the treasure in three parts, it will be not only a difficult sum, but less wealth for you and me."

"That is truth," agreed the other villain, "but when he returns he will demand his share."

"Not if we do as I plan. When he returns, you hold his arms as if you were hugging him in friendship. I will slip behind and stab him with my dagger."

But evil was running also in the mind of the third villain as he walked down the crooked road to the town. "Why should I divide this great treasure with those two ruffians?" he asked himself. "They were never anything to me. I would wish them dead before I would have them take two coins of every three in that green bag."

He began to plot how this foul deed could be done. "I will poison them," he decided. "I will buy a bottle of wine for each of us and put poison in two."

As he entered the town he saw an apothecary shop, where medicines and poisons were sold. "Friend," he said to the apothecary, "my house crawls with rats. Can you sell me a poison to kill them?"

"I can," he replied. "I have here a most deadly poison from the islands of the East. No one can drink so much as a drop without giving up life forever."

The young man bought enough poison to kill a

hundred men as bad as himself. Then he went to the baker for bread and to the vintner for wine. He bought three bottles, two green and one red. Into the green bottles he poured the poison. The red bottle he left clean and pure for his own drinking.

The young ruffian went back to his fellows, laughing to hide his villainy. They laughed to hide their own plan of murder. The traitorous one threw his arms around the youngest, calling him "dear friend." Then the oldest villain drew his knife and ran it into the heart of the youngest. He slipped to the earth without a sound.

"Let him lie till nightfall," said the smiler with the knife. Now let us eat and drink and be merry for the death of this ruffian."

They drew the cork from the red bottle and drank the wine. They ate the bread. Then they opened the two green bottles and raised them to their lips. They drank—and the bottles slipped from their hands, and they fell dead to the ground. Their eyes stared at the heavy black clouds and the branches of the green apple tree, but they did not see the sky or the tree. Nor did they see the little old man all in green, grinning at the three young men who had found Death in a green bag under a green apple tree.

The Witch
and Her Cow-milking Bag

Long ago in the time of the saints, there lived in England at the village of Brunne a holy man. People called him the "Bishop of Faith," because faith was what he talked about most of all.

But though he was a very holy man, he was a hard-hearted man, too. When rats came into the kitchen at night and ate a woman's bread, he did not scold the rats; he scolded the woman. When hail fell and crushed the corn in a farmer's field, he did not blame the weather; he blamed the man. "You were punished," he would say, "because you did not believe in what I told you. You have no faith."

A little girl with a broken doll, a little boy with a scraped knee—all heard the same words. "It is your fault. You were naughty children who didn't believe strongly in what I preached. You have no faith."

Those were the days when serpents still slithered in Ireland and witches still dwelt in England. But the time of the evil power of witches was gone. Most of the witches were old women who lived alone and did not trouble anyone. Of course, if a mischievous boy climbed through the hedges to steal her apples, a witch might shake her broomstick at him, and he would fall and skin his nose. People did not mind about that. "Serves him right," they would say. "Little boys should not steal apples."

Even though the witches were harmless, the Bishop of Faith did not like them. He said to the people of Brunne, "You must tell me who the witches are, and I will drive them out of the village." But sometimes the people did not tell him, because they felt sorry for the old witch women.

One witch who lived near Brunne was more troublesome than most. She refused to work for her daily bread. Instead she used her magic to steal food. She made a large bag out of leather and sewed it up so tightly that it would hold milk without leaking. Then she said some magic words and it came to life.

"I command you to hop," she told the bag. The bag hopped obediently along the floor, just like a trained dog. The witch clapped her hands with glee. "Now I shall have milk for my porridge, and not a penny to pay," she laughed.

Every morning before the sun rose she opened the door for the bag. "I command you to hop over to the pasture where the farmers' cows are. Milk the cows and bring the milk to me."

Every time she said the words, the bag hopped out of the door and across the fields to the neighbors' pasture. There it went from one cow to another, drawing the milk. Then it hopped back to the witch.

When the farmers came out to milk their cows, the cows were dry. "Some thief has been stealing our milk," they cried. "We must watch for him."

The farmers hid in the hedges and behind the barns, but they saw nothing, for they were looking for a thief with arms and legs and a head. They could not see the brown bag hopping quietly along, hidden in the darkness before dawn.

But one morning a heavy frost turned the grass of the pasture white as snow. Then they could see the bag. They watched it hop to the cows and draw the milk and hop away. They were not as frightened as you would be to see such a strange thing, because they had lived with witches for a long time. But they were angry. They followed the bag to see where it would go. As usual, it hopped home to the witch's house and bumped against the door till she let it in.

"That is too much for us to put up with," they said. "We must tell the Bishop of Faith." And so they did.

The Bishop had not caught a witch in a long time, and he decided to make an example of this one before all the people. He made the people of the village gather on the village green, and then he commanded the sheriff of Brunne to bring the witch before them.

"Wicked, wicked old woman!" he shouted. He shouted so loudly he could be heard all over the town and far beyond. "You have done an evil thing in charming a bag to steal milk. I will drive the evil power out of you." He preached so loud and long and hard that the people began to feel sorry for the witch.

"She is not so bad," they said. "If she has enough magic power to make a bag milk a cow, she could have done us great harm. But she only took milk for her porridge in the morning. How do we know the Bishop of Faith has more power than the witch? Perhaps he could not even make a bag hop along by itself. What has he ever done but tell us that we have no faith?"

The Bishop of Faith overheard this grumbling and decided to prove that his power was stronger than the power of the witch. He ordered the sheriff to bring the bag before him.

When the bag was on the ground, the Bishop of Faith said loudly, "Old woman! Say the words that make the bag come to life."

The witch said the magic words, and the bag rose up and moved around as if there were a pig inside it. The people cried out in wonder, and so they did not hear the Bishop tell the sheriff to copy down the magic words.

"Now make the bag hop around," said the Bishop to the witch.

The witch again said some magic words, and the bag began to dance. If you have ever seen a bag dance, you know how funny it is. The people all laughed, but the Bishop of Faith looked very stern.

"Silence!" he shouted. "This is not a laughing matter."

He took the paper from the sheriff. "Now," he said, "I will show you that I am stronger than the witch. I will make the bag come to life." And he said the same magic words that the witch had said.

But the bag lay on the ground as limp as an old coat that someone had thrown away.

"Bag!" shouted the Bishop. "I command you to hop!"

The bag lay still and quiet. The people began to giggle and laugh.

The Bishop of Faith turned red with anger. He shouted at the witch. "Evil old woman! Why is it that the bag came alive and moved when you said the words? Why did the bag lie still and quiet when I said the same words?"

The old woman's face was as brown and wrinkled and leathery as her bag, but it came to life when she grinned at the Bishop of Faith. She laughed in a squeaky cackle, as witches do.

"The bag came to life and hopped when I said the words because I believed in the words," she answered. "I had faith in what I said. You did not believe the words. You have no faith."

The Bishop turned and walked into his church. And ever afterward he was a better and nicer man, for he understood that most people are not saints, but just human beings like you and me.

Cunning Sean and the Dean

In the great city of Dublin stands Saint Patrick's Cathedral, the grandest church in all Ireland. Two hundred years ago this church had as its Dean a great and clever man who, like many other great and clever men, thought all other people were fools. He loved to play tricks on his poor servants until they complained, and then he would send them away without their wages. For in those days servants were not allowed to complain against their masters, and could lose their jobs if they did.

It was after he had discharged such an unfortunate fellow that a young man named Sean knocked upon his door. "Sean" is the Irish way of saying "John," you know. The Dean opened the door, and Sean bowed low and took off his cap very politely.

"May ye live all the days of your life," Sean said. "And would ye be wantin' a smart young lad for your servant?"

"I would indeed," replied the Dean, "but I'm a gruff master when a servant displeases me. Could you put up with the likes of that?"

"Sure and it would be grand to listen to ye when you're in a rage, such a great man ye be," smiled Sean. " 'Twould be a comfort to be cursed by ye."

"That's as well said as if I said it myself," said the Dean. "I'll give you a try. You shall live here in the cathedral and I'll feed you as fat as a puppy."

"And what would ye be payin' me for wages?" asked Sean.

"I'll pay you what you're worth," said the Dean.

"Sure and I can't live on that," Sean frowned.

"Ah," laughed the Dean, "you are a cunning lad. I'll make you a bargain. Work well for me without complaining for one whole year, and I'll give you enough money so that you will never have to be a servant again."

But Sean still frowned. "Great noise and little wool, as the devil said when he sheared the pig. I'm thinking there's a trick in ye."

"Never a trick," the Dean assured him. "But if you complain, out you go with nothing."

"Nowt?" asked Sean.

"Naught!" said the Dean.

"Ah," sighed Sean, "as the devil said to the porcupine, you're a very rough Christian. But I'll take the job if I might make one condition of me own. If I do everything ye tell me to do, but yet ye complain against me, then ye must give me the year's wages on the spot, and I'll be free to leave ye then and there."

"Done and done," laughed the Dean, for he was sure he could outwit Sean in any game he had a mind to play. "Well, Sean," he said, "you're on. You can begin by cleaning all the windows of the cathedral. Would you like a bite of breakfast first?"

"Sure and I would," answered Sean.

So the Dean had the cook bring in a big bowl of steaming oatmeal porridge, and lots of sugar, and hot homemade bread, and a big glass of milk.

"Now," said the Dean when Sean had finished eating, "there's not much sense in having to climb down the ladder from the windows just to have lunch, is there? So would you like a bite of lunch now?"

"I'm not complainin'," said Sean. "Bring it on and I'll see what I can do." So in came the cook again with a bowl of croodles. And if you don't know what croodles are, you are no Irishman.

"Sure and that was a good lunch," Sean said after

he had eaten the croodles. "Now I'll be off to me work."

The Dean came over and patted him on the shoulder. "Now, Sean, you're a good working lad. You wouldn't want to see the poor old cook come back tonight just to make your supper, would you? Just sit still and I'll have the cook put a bit of supper before you."

Sean's stomach was beginning to swell with all the porridge and bread and croodles that were in it. But when the meat and potatoes and potatoes and meat were brought in piping hot from the kitchen, he took up his knife and fork and went to it like the brave boy that he was.

He forked in the potatoes and he forked in the meat, and then he pushed his chair back from the table and put his hands on his stomach. "That's not a good fit, as the serpent said when he swallowed the billy goat. But I'm not complainin'."

"Good boy!" laughed the Dean. "Now you can go out and work hard all day without stopping, for you've had your breakfast, lunch, and supper, and there's not a thing in the world to stop for."

"Ah, no, Sorr," said Sean, shaking his head. "It's the law of the land that a serving man goes to bed after supper. And I've just had me supper. So good mornin' to ye, Sorr, and good day, and good night, and where's me bed? Wake me tomorrow in time for breakfast, and I'll have another good day's hard work."

"Ah, you rascal!" shouted the Dean. "You want to lie in bed all day, do you?"

"Indeed I do and indeed I will," anwered Sean. "Are ye complainin'?"

"No, I'm not complaining," the Dean muttered, for he did not want to give Sean a year's wages just for eating breakfast, lunch, and supper, all within the hour.

The next day the Dean woke Sean early and gave him breakfast—nothing else, you may be sure. "Take my horse to pasture," he ordered Sean, "and let him feed well on the sweet grass. And watch the horse every minute, for there are thieves about. If you don't watch the horse, I'll take the skin off you."

"Yes, Sorr," said Sean.

That night the Dean called Sean to him. "Saddle my horse," he ordered. "I must visit the Bishop."

"Ah, Sorr, that cannot be!"

"And why not, you rascal?"

"Ah, Sorr, it's because the robbers took your horse away and we'll never be seein' it again, I'm thinkin'."

"You blackguard!" roared the Dean. "Have they put the comether on you? Didn't I tell you to watch the horse?"

"So ye did, Sorr, and indeed I did. I watched the robbers come and take the horse and I watched them tie it to the back of their wagon and I watched them go over the hill. And then I ran to the top of the hill, so I did, and I watched them till they were out of sight. You're not complainin', Sorr, are ye?"

"I'm beginning to think I made a bad bargain with you, Sean, but I'm not complaining. You don't get a year's good wages out of me so easily."

One day the Dean decided to give a big dinner for the Bishop, and the Lord Mayor of Dublin and the Lord Mayor's lady, and all the rich merchants and important people. It would be the grandest and the gayest party of the year. The Dean hired a roomful of servants to help with dinner, but they were so foolish that he had to put Sean in charge of them.

"Let nothing go wrong tonight," warned the Dean, "or it will be the end of you. And don't you be jabbering to my guests. Hold your tongue and don't talk to the Bishop or the Lord Mayor. And warn those foolish servants to hold their tongues, too. Not a word out of any of you!"

That night the candles were lit in the great chandelier, and the lights sparkled on the rich glasses and on the rich silver knives and forks. The plates shone with the glow, and the damask tablecloth was the finest on any table in Dublin. The Lord Mayor was there with his lady, both dressed in their ermine gowns, and the Bishop was there, too, fine as any Bishop in the city. All the best people in Dublin sat around the table, talking and thinking about the fine dinner they would have.

And they talked. And they waited. And they waited. And they talked. But no dinner came. No servants appeared. No sound came from the kitchen.

The Dean squirmed in his chair at the head of the table. Finally his anger and his impatience were too much for him. "Sean!" he roared. "Come in here and bring those scoundrels of servants with you!"

The kitchen door was obediently opened and in they all came, one by one like soldiers in a parade, with Sean at the head, and all with their hands in their mouths. Silence fell over the guests.

"Are they all mad?" asked the Lord Mayor's lady.

"Sean, you rogue!" bellowed the Dean. "Where's the dinner?"

Sean took his hand out of his mouth. "Well, Sorr," he said, after sticking his tongue in and out of his

mouth a few times to loosen it up a bit, "there isn't any dinner. We all did just as ye told us. We held our tongues, and we couldn't hold our tongues and still use our hands to make the dinner. I can't understand why you'd want us to do such a silly thing as to hold our tongues, but we did as ye told us. But you're not complainin', are ye, Sorr?"

"Salvation seize your soul! You villain! Shouldn't I be complaining? The day I see the back of you for the last time will be the happiest day of my life!"

"Ah, Sorrs," said Sean to the Bishop and the Lord Mayor and the Lord Mayor's lady. "Ye hear well enough that the Dean is complainin' of his poor servant who never did but what he was told. The Dean has broken his bargain, and he must pay me the wages of a year and enough for me to be a master meself!"

A sad night it was for the Dean, for he had to pay Sean or be shamed before the whole city. It was a great bag of money he had to give his cunning servant, but he learned something worth all of it and more. He learned that poor fellows could be as clever as great fellows like himself. As for Sean, he lived as happily as anybody can with a bagful of gold and a headful of brains.

Glossary

aboon (uh BOON), above
alackaday (uh LAK uh day), a word that expresses sorrow
auld (awld), old
bairn (bayrn), a small child
baith (bayth), both
begorra (buh GAWR uh), a word that expresses surprise
bonnie (BON ee), beautiful
boob (boob), a foolish person
braw (braw), good, nice, handsome
canny (KAN ee), wise, careful
comether (kuh MEH thur), a charm
croodles (KROOD uhlz), bits of food in gravy
Da (dah), Dad, Father
daft (daft), crazy, foolish
dinna (DIN uh), do not
eejit (EE jit), idiot
gormless (GAWM lus), stupid, dull
guidman (GIHD man), goodman, husband
hae (hay), have
hech (hekh), a word that expresses hurt feelings
i' (ih), in
lawk-a-mercy (LAWK uh MUHR see), my heavens!
lobscouse (LOB skows), stewed meat and vegetables
loon (loon), a worthless, lazy person
maun (mawn), must
mon (mon), man
musha (MUSH uh), a word that expresses worry
notrocious (noh TROH shus), famous for being wicked
o' (oh), a short way to write *of* or *on*
och (okh), oh!
oot (oot), out
ould (ohld), old
sonsie (SON see), bringing good luck, lucky
sorr (suhr), sir
thochtless (THOKHT lus), thoughtless
tralliwaggers (TRAL uh wag urz), giants' food
tripes and **trullibubs** (tryeps and TRUL uh bubz), the insides of a giant
twa (twah), two
whisht (hwisht), hush!
wilna (WIL nuh), will not
ye (yee), you
yez (yeez), you (plural)

$9.51   #2235

398.2
GRE

Greenway, John
Tales from the
British Isles

DATE DUE			
4B	$5B	MAR 29	
MAY 3 4	OCT 27		
Smith			
5-A	NOV 17		
FEB 5			
R-5B	McBride		
MAR 1 8	CM		
L 5A	5A		
JAN 2 0	JAN 22		
DSB			
JAN 17	MAR 1 0		
Beihler			

398.2
Gre

$9.51   #2235

Greenway, John
Tales from the
British Isles